THE 9 POSITIVES

ACTUALIZE YOUR FULL POTENTIAL

Santosh Sachdeva

with

Tanushka Vaid

YogiImpressions®

YogiImpressions®

THE 9 POSITIVES
First published in India in 2015 by
Yogi Impressions LLP
1711, Centre 1, World Trade Centre,
Cuffe Parade, Mumbai 400 005, India.
Website: www.yogiimpressions.com

First Edition, April 2015
Revised Edition, March 2023

ISBN 978-93-94515-15-4

Contents

PREFACE

A lot has been said and written about positive thinking and positive affirmations in the past few years. So much so that it has started to sound like just a feel-good mantra or another way for people to boost their ego. Yet, somehow, despite all the skepticism surrounding these concepts, they refuse to fade away. The only explanation for this could be that they hold an inalienable truth at their very core.

The fundamental truth that holds the key to transforming our life is that the thoughts we think daily (about ourselves and the world around us) are shaping our life on a minute-to-minute basis. A case in point is an experiment that was conducted to determine the nature of light:

There were two groups of scientists: one believed

that light was made up of particles, and the other believed that light behaved as waves. They had gathered together in a lab to settle this matter once and for all. The first group conducted their experiment and proved that light comprises particles. Astonishingly, the second group also managed to prove their point that light behaves as waves. Everyone was shocked into silence. How could light be both?

Later, as quantum physics (the branch of science studying the smallest particles in the universe) developed, they went back to study the light experiment and discovered that light was reacting differently based on the expectations of the two groups studying its behavior. Because such a large group of scientists believed so strongly that light comprises particles, it behaved accordingly for them. And when an equally large, strongly opinionated group believed that light behaves as waves, it showed wave-like properties. Light adjusted itself in direct response to the thought waves (energy waves) being directed toward it.

Since light forms such an integral part of the universe and the basis for all life, we know that what is true for light is also true for all human life. The great sages of the East were right all along: once we learn how to direct our mind, we will be able to direct our world. And this is possible by wholeheartedly adopting the guidance provided in this book, *The 9 Positives.*

The Tibetan Connection

The Nine Positives are not just words or feel-good mantras. They are affirmations that can penetrate down to our cellular level if we practice them diligently. They are derived from teachings of breathing exercises and affirmations that have their roots in ancient Tibetan wisdom.

We are fortunate to have access to these Tibetan gems because of an Englishman named John Dingle. Many decades ago, he was magnetically drawn to Tibet where he studied these exercises under revered Tibetan monks and, in time, came to be known as Ding Le Mei. Eventually, he moved back to the West and became the link that drew these sacred teachings out of Tibet and into the rest of the world.

Ding Le Mei compiled the knowledge of the lamas (Tibetan Buddhist monks) into a structured course that he shared with students far and wide through the establishment of the Institute of Mental Physics in California, USA. This course found its way to India and was renamed 'Brahma Vidya — Knowledge of Creation.' The course consists of a set of eight breathing exercises along with their respective affirmations.

The Nine Positives are part of the affirmations for the second breathing exercise, and according to some people, form the bedrock of the entire Brahma Vidya Course.

How Can This Book Help Us?

Usually, we live our life through the lens of our past experiences, memories, conditioning, and data. For example, if a dog bit you when you were young, you would most likely be scared of dogs even when you were older. Our life is a mixture of good as well as not-so-good experiences. However, for most of us, our strongest memories — the ones we can't easily forget or let go of — tend to be painful, such as that of a person who betrayed us. We may refrain from constantly thinking about those situations or people, but these memories remain stored in our subconscious mind.

And unbeknownst to us, it is our subconscious mind that guides our life. This is why we keep attracting similar people and situations, such as abusive relationships or financial troubles, which we (in our external life) are trying so hard to get out of. Think of it as an iceberg; the part that is visible to us is only the tip (what we term as our 'mind'), but the majority of the iceberg lies below our line of sight, in the depth of the ocean (in this case, our subconscious mind). So, to change our life, we need to work on both — our conscious mind and our subconscious mind.

Over time, as we practice The Nine Positives, they get imbibed into our subconscious mind and slowly undo all the conditioning and negative patterns that we have accumulated, not just in this life but also in our previous ones. It is important that these affirmations are practiced in the order that they are given as the benefit derived from each one paves the way for the effective practice of the subsequent ones. All of them are linked together; hence, the end result is synergistic.

Thus, by systematically rewiring our mind and body to seek light instead of being lost in the darkness of our past pain, we can take back our power to manifest a life of beauty, passion, and pride. And the next time we are faced with a difficult situation, these affirmations will spring up automatically (if we have been sincere in our practice) to give us the guidance and support we need to thrive in life.

Santosh Sachdeva

Mumbai, 2023

INTRODUCTION

In his book *Voices from the Heart,* His Holiness the Dalai Lama succinctly explains mankind's fundamental raison d'être: "The purpose of life is to be happy." However, those of us who have lived long enough to see life in all its colors realize that happiness does not come without effort. To achieve that blissful state of mind, we have to learn how to direct our mind instead of allowing our mind to direct us. One of the most effective resources to guide the mind in the direction we want is through the use of confident, truthful, and firm statements, also known as positive affirmations. Just as we keep emphasizing the points we would like our young children to learn, or repeat commands to teach our puppies how to behave, through affirmations, we vocalize the words we would like our mind to imbibe and internalize.

Does this mean, then, that affirmations are simply a tool to train our mind? Or can they impact our lives personally and collectively as well? My mentor, Justice M. L. Dudhat (who taught the Brahma Vidya course in Mumbai, India), would emphasize time and again: "Every thought has a form and the potential to actualize itself."

This means that the Universe is continuously responding to the signals we send out and determining our future accordingly. If this seems a bit unbelievable, try to think of a time when you noticed how miserable people seemed to attract more misery or those who were successful kept attracting more success. Did it seem unfair? Or is it fair that the Universe gives each of us exactly what we focus most of our attention on?

In a traditional Indian household, whenever a negative word is uttered by someone, they are immediately admonished by others with the words '*Shubh-shubh bolo* (Speak positive, auspicious words)!' The wisdom that if we speak positively, we manifest positivity, and the other way around, has been with us for ages. But we only imbibe it when we're ready to act on it.

Connecting with the Universe

This book presents The Nine Positives, gems of ancient Tibetan wisdom that can lead you to a deeper understanding of yourself and the relationship you share with Consciousness as a whole.

In his book *The Power of Your Subconscious Mind,* Dr. Joseph Murphy gives us instructions on how to direct the mind:

1. Think about people as you would want them to think about you.
2. Feel about people as you would want them to feel about you.
3. Act toward people as you would want them to act toward you.

You may have also heard it said another way: "What goes around, comes around." The sayings are many, the truth is the same — send out (not just through your actions but also through your words and thoughts) only that which you would want to receive. Most of us think that we interact with the world solely through the medium of our actions or our words. This stems from our belief that no one is listening to our thoughts. But the Universe is always listening. As mentioned in the light experiment in the previous chapter, although the scientists were unaware that light would behave in response to their thoughts, they discovered much later that it was reflecting their mind. Similarly, we may think that our life and the people in it are unaffected by the 'secrets' of our mind, but, in reality, our situations are reflecting our thoughts.

Furthermore, when our mind, body, thoughts, and emotions are in alignment, we multiply our power and ability to communicate with the Universe. This is because we can consciously choose and decide what we want to send out to the Universe and, consequently, what it is we want to be reflected to us. Usually, this process happens without us having any conscious control over it.

However, this does not mean that we can simply dream up or imagine improbable situations in our head — such as winning a million-dollar lottery or marrying a superstar — and expect the Universe to fulfill them. We must also let our reason endorse whatever we imagine. The deep conviction of achieving what is desired has to pass from the mental state (after your reason has endorsed it) into the state of feeling so that we not only *feel* the outcome to be a certainty but also *know* it to be a certainty.

Wise men, like Dr. Murphy, say that there are three stages to creating and manifesting all that we aspire to in our life:

First, we think.

Second, we feel.

Third, we act.

This means that there is a law that determines the outcome of all that we aspire to.

The first part, thinking, involves both imagining and reasoning, as mentioned above. While imagining gives the thoughts their creative faculty, it is reasoning that determines the certainty of the thoughts coming to pass.

The second part, feeling, is what translates the mental vibrations into tangible emotions that we can feel in our body. For example, you may have a gut feeling that something positive or negative is going to happen.

When we take the third step of acting, keeping in our mind and emotions the conviction of seeing our desires fructify, then everything we do gets magnified by the forces of the Universe.

Let us understand all three stages with the help of an example: Imagine the type of house (its size, design, and location) you would like for yourself in the future while keeping in mind reasonable constraints of time, finances, and practicality. As you think more about it, you start to get a strong gut feeling that it is practical and achievable. Once you have your whole plan in place and you know it will work, then you can start to act on building your house, and in time, see your plan fructify.

But it is not easy to keep positive thoughts, dreams, or ideals anchored in our mind when we are facing the tides of negativity, misfortune, or constant disappointments. This is because our untrained mind is wired to oscillate between the dead past and an imaginary future (which is subconsciously a reflection of our past experiences). Most of our thoughts remain negative — 'I can't,' 'It's impossible,' or 'It won't happen' — and they seem to be proven right even when we are trying desperately in our conscious mind to believe otherwise.

To counter this, there is a lot of emphasis on silencing the mind. But what if we could simply rewire it instead? Then, perhaps, we could teach ourselves to live in the present, where joyfulness, hope, and peace reside. Once this is achieved, mastery over ourselves and our life will give us the freedom from becoming slaves to circumstances.

Those who believe in destiny may argue that everything is predetermined and that we cannot escape the cards we've been dealt in life. However, the approach of a modern seeker (like ourselves) is different; we believe that there must be a way to circumvent or bring about a positive change in our circumstances. Even if an unfavorable situation arises or persists, a change in our attitude toward it has the power of changing the way we view our life as a whole. Once we are in control of our mind and reactions, we will be well prepared to meet every situation or circumstance that arises in daily living. If we are efficient in dealing with our personal life with the right understanding, a firm will, decisiveness, and equanimity, no situation in life or any thought about the future can overwhelm us.

Once we have learned the art of circumventing and managing unpleasant situations and circumstances, we can then move toward manifesting the life we aspire for.

I AM

The saying "What you seek is also seeking you" means that we merely have to learn how to align ourselves to the vibration of the frequencies we aspire to and want to attract in life. To help us do this, the ancient Tibetan sages have given us The Nine Positives. These aim to bring forth in us the hidden qualities of our being so that we can manifest them in our day-to-day life.

Each affirmation starts with the words 'I am.' This is significant because 'I am' is mentioned in the scriptures of different religions as an expression of God. The Hindu scriptures say "*Aham Brahmasmi* [I am Brahman]." The words 'I am' represent eternal existence, namely, the past, the present, and the future.

In these *mahavakyas* (great sayings), the words 'I am' are followed by a quality that is the true nature of our Highest Self. Very often, we keep searching for these qualities in the external world, but they lie elusively hidden within our depths. The nine affirmations will help these qualities arise in us and manifest themselves in our life.

We have to let these affirmations reveal themselves to us. This is possible if, with childlike wonder and surrender, we make them a part of our life.

By repeating the affirmations before the start of our day and as the last thing we do before we fall asleep every night, they become a *mantra*, which will get internalized and arise of its own accord when required. In time, if we are sincere in our practice, their deeper meaning will begin to unfold, and a more fulfilling, nurturing, prosperous life will blossom in its wake.

The First Positive

1

I AM WHOLE

What Does 'Wholeness' Mean?

We, as individuals, are simultaneously a part of the whole universe and the whole universe condensed into a single part. Think of it this way: a drop of water from the ocean is both a part of the ocean and has the substance of the whole ocean in a part.

We live in this universe along with other species, animate and inanimate, in a process of mutual give and take, thereby creating harmony in the functioning of the totality. We are linked together with the rest of Creation through an invisible yet indivisible thread of consciousness. The moment we consider ourselves isolated from others, disruption takes place.

This can be seen in the evolution of our world

through the centuries. Earlier, though we lived in jungles, with only the bare necessities and no technology, we treated the wildlife and nature around us with respect. In return, the wild animals, by and large, also stayed out of our huts and settlements. But today, we constantly try to meddle with nature by cutting down forests, pushing back the sea, and endangering animal species. Consequently, in some places, incidents of leopards walking into settlements or elephants stomping down villages, or an increase in global wildfires and tsunamis have taken place at an alarming rate.

As long as we believed in wholeness and the oneness of the world, taking only what we needed and giving back in equal measure, our life was also whole. Earlier, we didn't have the kind of stress that modern man has: we didn't need pills for our anxiety or therapy for our depression. But once we believed the world was fragmented and we could exploit individual aspects of it without any dire consequences, then slowly, our life started to mimic that, and we too became fragmented, with a broken heart and an unfulfilled life.

The universe is governed by the laws of Consciousness. Consciousness is the fabric of energy that makes up all existence. Since it is one, it treats every aspect of itself with oneness. Think of it this way: You have different organs in your body that work together for the functioning of the whole body. These organs are treated fairly but not equally. For example, your digestive system may need more blood to help it perform its function than the endocrine system does. But this doesn't mean that your heart loves your digestive system more and so supplies more blood to it. It simply means that it knows what is required for each organ and serves it accordingly.

Similarly, when life gives you more of a particular thing (such as success), it does not mean that it loves you more. It just means that life knows what is best for each one of us at each moment.

If we saw ourselves as an intricate part of the whole world instead of separate from it, we would realize that every individual has their role in life (just as every organ has a different function) and everyone is contributing in their own way to fulfill the larger purpose of life — our collective spiritual growth.

The laws of Consciousness ensure that everything moves to a set rhythm. We observe this phenomenon in all of nature: seasons change automatically one after the other, birds follow their typical periods of migration, prey is hunted down by bigger animals and replaced at a steady rate, and flowers grow according to the environment they are in. Originally, we humans had our place and part in this cosmic dance, and we lived accordingly.

However, we were also equipped with the best (and arguably the worst) gift of nature — free will. Over generations and lifetimes, we isolated ourselves from the world and tried to impose our individual will on the whole of Creation. To do this, we had to break out of our native state of wholeness and believe the lie that we could progress even at the detriment of others.

With this understanding, when we say "I am

whole," it means that we are returning to our roots and once again coming into balance or alignment with the whole.

People often crave more fullness in their life; they feel that their life or relationships are fragmented or lacking in something. When we say "I am whole," we are reaffirming that everything we need (to make our life full) lies within us. Because when something is whole, it means that nothing is lacking, and everything is fully in balance. And once you are in balance, everything in your external life will also be in balance.

Are We Really Whole?

Wholeness is within us. If we project a thought of wholeness into our inner space, it is bound to bear fruit. Even though we may feel fragmented, when we choose to say "I am whole," what we are doing is we are planting the seed for wholeness. Each time we repeat the statement, we are reaffirming the seed we have planted in our mind. Hence it is important that we say the affirmation in the present tense.

Science has proved that if we were to take even a single atom (the basic building block of all Creation) and remove it from the world, the entire world would crumble. If we think of how many billions of atoms each one of us is made up of, we will realize what an integral part of the world we all are.

We are whole, and the entire universe, of which we are a part, is whole. The universe exists because we exist. Once we can imbibe this, we will never feel fear, doubt, or apprehension again.

'I am whole' is further explained as 'Nothing is lacking in us, and nothing can be added to us.' If something is whole, the question of something lacking does not arise. Nothing can be given to the universe (us) because everything already belongs to the universe (us).

Very often, something that takes us away from our sense of wholeness is our experience of sorrow. We think that in a perfect life, there would be no pain, struggle, or failure. So when we are faced with difficult situations in life, we become fragmented; we start scrambling to fix everything in a desperate need to make our life whole again. However, this is not necessary or true.

To be whole means that we are living our life to the fullest. This does not mean it is only a life full of fun and frolic. It means that we are experiencing all the emotions which make up life, whether it is pleasure, pain, sorrow, joy, envy, or any other emotion. We are experiencing a full life — the good along with the not-so-good.

From this perspective, we can look at life with a new awareness in which we neither accept nor reject anything and understand it all as a play of Consciousness. This means that we realize that all situations in our life are being sent our way to help us grow. We don't need to change life or ourselves; it is already whole, as are we.

We may wonder how everything in life can simultaneously be whole. Something should be a part, right? There is a beautiful Sanskrit chant from the Upanishads that explains this. I encourage you to contemplate it and recite it daily if it resonates with you.

Om Purnamadah Purnamidam
Purnaat purnamudachyate
Purnasya purnamaadaaya purnamevaavashishsyate
Om Shanti Shanti Shanti

Om, that is wholeness, this is wholeness
From wholeness comes wholeness
Though this wholeness is taken from that
  wholeness
This wholeness remains whole
Om, peace, peace, peace

Method of Visualization

While in a relaxed state of mind, contemplate the word 'whole.' An image or a sensation of roundness will probably come to your mind. Think outwards from the mind, and you will sense that roundness expanding. Now, try to feel this roundness and wholeness. Lose yourself in it so that in the expansion, as thought ceases, you experience yourself in the expanded state of blissful wholeness. When you say the affirmation 'I am whole,' it has to be said with a strong feeling of conviction and in a firm voice for it to be effective.

Over time, as you repeat the affirmation, you will realize the difference it has made in your daily life from the way you conduct yourself, your relationships, and the situations you face.

The Second Positive

2

I AM PERFECT

What Does 'Perfection' Mean?

Often, our interpretation of 'perfection' would mean not having any flaws, always saying and doing the right thing, and having nothing in life that is out of place. A simple introspection of human life would then reveal that none of us fit this definition of perfection.

A deeper interpretation of the term, however, would look at our internal life instead of our external one because it is that which makes up the foundation of who we really are. To be perfect, in that sense, would be to be someone always ready to learn to grow, love, give, and expand since these are the qualities of our inner being, which constantly wants to move closer to the light.

No matter who we may be on the surface or what limits we place on our capabilities, we all harbor these qualities of perfection within us, and we are calling them to the forefront with the affirmation 'I am perfect.'

We interact with the outside world as if we are beggars, begging for love, attention, recognition, or respect. This may sound harsh, but if we were to be brutally honest with ourselves, we would see that most human relationships are based on the expectation that 'you make me (my ego) feel good, and I will make you (your ego) feel good.' And when we interact with ourselves, we think, *Oh! I am no good. Look at so-and-so. I will never be as good as she is.*

The affirmation 'I am perfect' helps us change this narrative. To be perfect means that when we interact with ourselves, we recognize ourselves as beings worthy of love, kindness, and respect. We cherish our inner being that is so desperately seeking approval and validation. And once we know that we are inherently beings worthy of a perfect life, when we interact with others, we will, in fact, be humbler, kinder, and more loving toward them. Because we will have recognized that all of us (and all of life) are perfect *as is*.

The only thing we chase more than perfection in our being is probably perfection in our external life, such as the perfect house, car, spouse, children, or job. For years, movies have been selling us the idea that something is perfect only if it doesn't have any problems. But in reality, it is problems that challenge us, guide us, and motivate us. So a lack of motivation or a lack of problems would, in that sense, be a lack of life itself.

"We are not human beings having a spiritual experience; we are spiritual beings having a human experience." This quotation points to the fact that all situations, people, and experiences that we encounter are especially designed to help us grow and recognize the innate perfection of life.

As humans, we often put conditions, judgments, and timelines on events, and when they don't live up to our standards or expectations, we lament about what a mess our life or the world is. But everything in life happens at the right time, with the right people, and in the right place. When we look back on our life, we can see that the situations in our life were not really in our control; the only thing we could control was our reaction to them. We can choose to become or remain brave and kind people, and deal with adversity to the best of our ability.

Sometimes we notice that the more we resist a particular person or event, the more it seems to persist in our life; if we learn from it, then over time, the situation or person no longer bothers us anymore and may even go away on its own. This is because the universal intelligence puts us in a particular environment or a situation, not as a punishment but rather as an opportunity for growth. It provides us with relationships and experiences meant to help us grow into wiser, happier, nicer people. Therefore, it is best to accept each situation that we find ourselves in and learn the lesson that each experience has to teach us. This is the way to reach external perfection and spiritual progress.

When we support life in its endeavor to make us grow, and recognize our innate perfection, then we reduce our need to go through the same situations repetitively and move toward liberation.

Are We Really Perfect?

Usually, when we call ourselves 'perfect,' we think we are being egoistic or presumptuous. This is because a traditional definition of 'perfect' is reached by excluding everyone else, as if to say "I am perfect but you are not. So you need to change, or the situation needs to change."

However, from a different and holistic perspective, we can think of a jungle as an example of perfection, as its ecosystem is harmonious and whole within itself. Similarly, true perfection wouldn't mean that we are better than the rest; it would mean that we are in harmony with the rest of Creation and whole within ourselves.

Perfection doesn't mean matching certain criteria

or preset standards; it means being true to our inner self and marching to a different drummer. The more we trust our perfection and the intelligence that made (and continues to govern) this whole universe, the more our external life will start to replicate this inner state of perfection.

Method of Visualization

When you think of the word 'perfect,' the sensation in your mind will be different from that which you experience when you think of the word 'whole.' You may visualize a key that fits into a lock perfectly, a dancer who moves exactly in rhythm with the music, a still lake near the mountains, a newborn baby, or anything that represents the word 'perfect' for you.

As you focus on that visual, think about how calm your mind feels while looking at it. For once, don't try to judge, comment on, or influence the image. It is perfect, in a sense, because your mind doesn't try to make it otherwise. If it looked for imperfection, it would probably find it. Similarly, you too are perfect. The more you silence or rewire your mind (through The Nine Positives), the more you will be able to recognize and relate to this fact.

If you are whole, you are automatically bound to be perfect since imperfection comes when something is lacking within you. As you visualize and affirm "I am perfect," you will invite and uncover more perfection in your life.

In the morning, start by reciting "I am whole." You may do this in the open or in front of a window or a mirror. Go through the visualization for wholeness. Take your time and don't be in a rush. Then follow it up with the next affirmation, 'I am perfect,' and the corresponding visualization. Similarly, as you progress, you must do each of the nine affirmations with their accompanying visualizations in the correct order every morning.

The Third Positive

3

I AM STRONG

What Does 'Strength' Mean?

When we say 'strong' we are not only talking about physical strength but also, more importantly, about mental, emotional, and moral strength. To put it simply, strength is the ability to deal with a situation in the way that is required, to the best of our abilities. It may mean emotional strength when a loved one passes away, mental strength to walk away from situations or people that are pulling us down, physical strength to lift weights at the gym, or moral strength to stand up for what is right and best for us.

Strength comes from within — from the thoughts we have at each moment. For example, you would have heard of someone performing an incredible feat, such as a young girl swimming in the sea, against the current, from one dock to the other; the first woman from India who wrestled professionally; or the boy who didn't let a severe injury stop him from competing athletically. In most of these cases, you would have heard the participants proudly declare, "No one thought I would be able to do it. But I had made up my mind to prove them wrong, so I did." Here is the key: while their size, age, and circumstances may have all worked against them, simply by the strength of their mind, they were able to overcome all adversities and perform wonders. On the other hand, you would have also heard of world-famous gymnasts pulling back from the Olympics because of mental health reasons or footballers missing a penalty because of overwhelming mental pressure. This is the opposite scenario where these people may have circumstances in their favor, but a moment of weakness in their mind causes them to miss out on opportunities.

Whether we know it or not, every thought we think comes with a force to fulfill our intentions.

This is explained in the previous chapters in the words of Dr. Murphy, who said that if we first *think* a thought strongly, we can consequently *feel* it strongly in our body, and then if we *act* upon it, our actions get magnified by the strength of our mind.

Thoughts have a magnetic power; they attract similar thoughts one after the other, and the subsequent force generated through them is strong enough to change the outcome of a situation in the external world. For example, a friend tells you that a person named Alex said something negative about you. You feel hurt and wonder why Alex would say something like that. Then your thoughts go back to other instances where Alex hurt you or someone else. You perhaps think, *Enough is enough. I will give him a piece of my mind.* Then you start to think of all the things you will say to him when you meet him. When you finally see Alex, you accuse him of saying something negative about you behind your back and ask him if the accusation is true. While you superficially may pretend to give him a chance to explain, you both know that you are not interested in the explanation and just want to hurt him. Alex senses your hostility and reacts badly to it. Any chance of the whole situation being a misunderstanding or miscommunication, and being resolved amicably, has been wiped out.

In the above example, you can see how the thought 'Why would he say that?' led to so many similar thoughts of negativity, to which Alex lashed out in defensiveness. Compare this to a situation where you had decided not to think or say anything to Alex until you honestly, openly heard his side of the story. Then the situation and the relationship could have been saved.

Similarly, when you say the affirmation 'I am strong,' you are sending out those thought waves into the universe. When strength is required in a particular moment, the required strength will get magnified to help you achieve whatever you set out to.

Are We Really Strong?

Are we really strong? Yes, we are. Life only gives us as much as we can deal with — not more, not less. And before sending any person or situation our way, it will first send us all the resources and strength we need to excel in each experience.

No matter how weak or incapable we may feel from time to time, even on days when the tears don't stop, or even when hoping for change seems difficult, we carry an inner reservoir of immense strength that no person or situation can ever deplete. If we reflect on our life or the stories of those around us, we will remember times when we thought that there was no way we would survive or ever be happy again, for instance, when we lost a loved one or a job, or had to break off a relationship. However difficult it may have been, we eventually moved past it because of our strength. The strength and support may have also come externally in the form of friends, mentors, or signs. These were gifts that life gave to help us get through that situation.

If we feel that we still need more help, we can manifest more strength into our life for ourselves. All that is required for us to feel strong is for us to tap into ourselves by affirming "I am strong," believing it, and allowing it to magnify in all spheres of our life. Let's take an example of physical strength: Imagine a nine-year-old girl carrying her disabled teenage brother out of the house in case of a fire. People may be left wondering where she got the strength to perform such a daring feat. The strength came from within her and emerged in response to the need of the circumstances.

In the same way, all difficult situations act as a catalyst to pull out strength from within us.

If we take time to reflect, we will notice that in any situation, a thought arises first, then the feeling, and then the action. So we should always affirm "I am strong." With this, the tremendous strength that we start feeling begins to reflect in our personality, and the required action follows.

Method of Visualization

When you think of the word 'strong,' feel the sensation that arises in your mind and extend it to your body. This is important because it will be in accordance with the image of strength that you identify with. For example, you may think of a lion or an elephant, or even immobile forms of nature such as a mountain or an oak tree. Keep this visual (of the lion or mountain or whatever your choice of image is) at the forefront of your mind, think of the word 'strength,' and repeat the affirmation 'I am strong' over and over again. Feel yourself merge into that image and become one with it. For example, you may view yourself as a lion, roaring at the challenges in your life and knowing that you will overcome them, or as a mountain, standing firm even as the difficult storms of life rage around you.

You don't need anything externally. Everything you need is within you and will manifest from within you. Thus, you realize that you are whole, perfect, and also strong.

When you continue to say "I am strong" repeatedly, over time, you will find tremendous strength developing within you in any situation, such as taking a walk, communicating, working, or exercising. A certain confidence starts developing in you and gives you the strength you need. With the thought of strength, a tangible feeling of being strong will also arise in your mind and body. Once your thoughts and emotions arc in alignment, you will automatically start to act as well as interact from a position of strength.

Repeat the affirmations and visualizations for 'whole' and 'perfect' first, before carrying them out for 'I am strong.'

The Fourth Positive

4

I AM POWERFUL

What Does 'Power' Mean?

To be truly powerful means to have complete control over our mind-body organism. Often, we associate power with being able to make changes in the world outside us. But that would happen automatically if we simply knew how to, and had the power to, make changes *inside* us. This knowledge — of change taking place from inside to outside — stems from our understanding of the fact that the entire world is merely a projection of our inner space. Think of it this way: A poor old man on the road laments about how life is miserable and how everyone is a thief. An honest politician looks at the world and sees only problems that he needs to solve, and a teacher sees only students who need to be taught. A spiritual master talks about compassion and happiness. Technically, all these people are living in the same world — Planet Earth. But experientially, all of them are living in different worlds. More often than not, depending on their inner state, they may be living in kind worlds, mean worlds, harsh worlds, or gentle worlds. Even two people born in the same family and raised the same way grow up to look at the world differently.

This means that the only way to view the world is through the lens of how we view ourselves, and subsequently, the only power to change the world comes from the power of having changed ourselves. In essence, very often, a kind person will manifest an equally kind world for themself, whereas an unkind person will encounter an unkind world every step of the way.

We may think, *Oh! But I'm so kind. So why do unkind things still happen to me?* This is where power comes in. Is there power in our kindness, love, or acceptance? Or is there weakness? For example, a housewife may not react to the taunts of her husband because she is too scared to raise her voice at him and face the consequences of his wrath. Or a child may let a bully eat their lunch because they are afraid of confronting them. In these cases, their complacency is not a sign of acceptance or love. It does not arise from a position of power; it arises from weakness.

Now take an example of a senior who knows that their new subordinate has made a mistake. They know that if the boss finds out, the subordinate will be fired. So they take the blame on themself because they know it won't have any repercussions for them the way it will have for their subordinate. In this case, their kindness and generosity come from power. Similarly, if a wife feels empowered enough to tell her husband off but holds back because he's had a difficult day at the office and would rather discuss it tomorrow, or a child shares their food with their friend who forgot to carry lunch, then it is, once again, a case of love coming from power and not from weakness.

We may try to cover up our weakness, fear, or

hesitancy and pass it off as acceptance or kindness, but we can't fool life. It sees how unkind we are being to ourselves, in a sense, by not standing up for what is right and reflects that unkindness to us so that we realize this and change our ways.

We can call upon the reservoirs of power hidden deep within us to change ourselves and our patterns of being, and, in effect, change our life and our world.

The difference between strength and power, for me, is that being strong is the ability to face every situation the way it is and come out shining. Whereas being powerful is the ability to change the course of the situation for the future in a way that works best for all of us. Think of it this way: If you lose a family member in a road accident due to a faulty signal, you will need immense strength to deal with the tragedy and go through the period of mourning. You may then decide that no other family will have to suffer like yours did and decide to take action. You may file petitions, organize protests, run for local office — do anything you can do to ensure the faulty signal gets replaced by an accurate one. These actions you take to prevent future accidents show your power.

Both these qualities are important in their own way because they enable us to accept what we can't change and try to change what we can't accept.

When we think of power, qualities like self-confidence and decisiveness also come to mind. At times, a strong will or determination can help us shoulder immense responsibility and even overcome physical weakness, if any, to generate an explosion of energy.

Are We Really Powerful?

The universe is an unlimited source of power. Everything in the macrocosm (cosmos) is expressed in the microcosm (each human). Therefore, the microcosm has within itself all the counterparts of the macrocosm as potential, ready to actualize them whenever the situation arises.

We have seen the power that Nature has; it can bring the entire world to its knees. Nothing can meet the sheer power and force of Mother Nature once She chooses to unleash it. We have seen this with countless tsunamis, volcanoes, and most recently, the COVID-19 pandemic. Conversely, we also experience the gentler power of Mother Nature when she makes a beautiful flower blossom from a crack in the wall or when we see a lioness taking care of an abandoned cub or a crow taking twigs to build a sturdy nest. Then we realize that power can be expressed in different ways.

Nothing indeed is as powerful as a mother's love because, when her child is in danger, a mother forgets any limitations she may have thought she had and stands up to defend her child. In doing so, she lets go of her weaknesses and connects to the power of the universe (by the sheer force of her will), and channels that energy through her to face the situation and make her child safe again. This same energy can be consciously channeled by all of us. Think of it this way: Your body has trillions of cells producing over a trillion reactions per second. Each and every cell in your body is like a power plant generating high-voltage energy. When you allow the potential of these cells to work for you, then you are functioning at your highest potential. By repeated vocalization of the affirmation 'I am powerful,' you call upon this power to rise from the depth of your being.

With the above understanding and awareness, whenever the thought arises within you to actualize a particular aspect of your personality, it is bound to manifest itself.

Method of Visualization

As with the earlier affirmations, think about what 'power' means to you and then see what symbol it brings to your mind. It is very important that you *feel* the meaning of the word, and not just *think* of a symbol of power.

You may also think of an instance or experience that made you feel powerful. You may visualize yourself standing on top of a mountain, having conquered your fear of heights; standing up to the bully at the office; or giving a presentation after having overcome your stage fright. Visualize yourself standing proud, happy, and confident in these situations. You know that you are whole, perfect, strong, and powerful. Practice the affirmations and visualizations in the same order.

The word 'power' implies that for whatever you do, you have a sufficient supply of power required to fulfill your purpose. This is why you should affirm "I am powerful," so that you can draw power from the depths of your being and manifest it into the world.

The Fifth Positive

5

I AM LOVING

What Does 'Love' Mean?

Think of love, of its changeless nature, and its essence, in whatever form it presents itself to your mind. There are many different aspects to love: it may be requited or unrequited, and it may be toward other people, animals, places, or objects. Each type of love mentioned above has a unique nature of its own, and even within each category, the essence of love differs. For example, when it comes to loving other people, the way you love your parents is different from the way you love your friends, and both of these are different from the way you love your romantic partners. Or the way you love the Eiffel Tower in Paris will not be the same as the way you love your childhood home.

Sometimes, love may make us stronger than we ever thought possible, and at other times, it may lay bare our weaknesses for everyone to see. Love is the emotion that can give us the greatest joy as well as make us experience the most tragic pain. It is the nectar we so desperately crave; yet, often, we are so afraid to fully taste it. Because the only way to truly experience love is to lose ourselves in it; to allow ourselves to be fully vulnerable, open, and receptive; to not allow our fear of heartbreak, judgment, or rejection to put any barriers between us and the object of our love; and to be willing to be less so that our love may prevail.

The love that we understand in ordinary parlance is from the preconceived notions that we have developed, right from the time we were born up to this moment. Movies usually portray only the type of love that takes place between a man and a woman in a relationship. The concept of 'true love' has been used so often and with such careless disregard, that we cringe when we hear it. It depicts love only as a problem-free and happily-ever-after relationship between a man and a woman.

Does this mean that the concept of true love itself is false? Or is it only our understanding of the term that is faulty?

Spiritual master Mirra Alfassa, known as The Mother, says, "Love is self-giving without asking anything in return." So often for us, even love has become a transaction. We may tell our children or spouses, "I do so much for you, so you must also do something for me." Or we think, *I love playing badminton so much, but I must also win tournaments. Otherwise, it is a waste of time.* Even before we have given, we are looking to see what we will get in return. The Mother advises us against this. She asks us to give ourselves fully — our time, effort, energy, or joy — without asking for anything, not even love, in return.

We may find ourselves asking "Well, if I'm not going to get anything in return, why would I choose to love? What is the point?" And therein lies the secret: the point of love is love itself. When channeled correctly, it is the expression of love that raises us to the peaks of happiness, success, and Consciousness.

Think of it this way: Have you seen a new mother hold her baby right after delivery? She has just been through hours of excruciating pain, the baby has done nothing for her but cry, and she knows she has long nights ahead of her. And yet, is she angry? Or is she absolutely elated? In that one moment, she has touched true love. This can also be seen in people who cherish their pets, knowing that their dog won't ever be able to make them breakfast, or in people who go play a sport they love despite knowing they will never be as good as professional athletes. It is the joy in loving (whether it's a baby, an animal, or an activity) that refreshes and rejuvenates them.

This type of love may be difficult for us to understand and, perhaps, even more difficult for us to practice. But this is the type of love we need to aim for if we want our love for everyone and anyone to become a means for bringing us closer to Consciousness.

Unconditional love is best expressed through nature. Nature gives of itself without any discrimination, without expecting anything from us in return. God has created everything for a purpose, and all Creation moves in harmony to fulfill that purpose. For example, the nature of the mango tree is to produce mangoes. While somebody nurtures the tree, another person plucks its fruit. However, when the time comes to bear fruit, the tree does not differentiate between the two people. It remains true to its nature of giving without discrimination.

Everything in nature moves to the rhythm of love and harmony so that perfect order is maintained. *This* is love. When love expresses itself for the sake of love, then, in that moment, the presence of God or bliss is experienced.

Are We Really Loving?

Are we really loving? To put it simply — yes. The entire world is an expression of love: the Divine's Love for us and our Love for Him (whether we associate the Divine as 'God,' nature, or our Highest Self). If someone were to ask "How can I experience infinity?" the answer would be "Only through love."

On the surface, we may have put many barriers

that prevent us from experiencing and expressing love in our daily life. They may be there to prevent us from getting hurt, feeling vulnerable, or being rejected. However, when we block love, we are also blocking joy, spontaneity, courage, and compassion. But it is only our love — for our children, life, humanity, or truth — that makes us wake up and face each new day despite everything we have endured.

The affirmation 'I am loving' brings us back to our core and the realization that, in the end, love makes our world go round.

Method of Visualization

When you say the word 'love,' what is the feeling it elicits in you? Is it one of belonging, togetherness, and peace? Let yourself feel the love and all the emotions it brings along with it.

You may visualize yourself cuddling a pet, sitting by the ocean, enjoying a cup of tea with a friend, or taking a long walk with a loved one. Keep that image in your mind as you start to experience the warm, fuzzy feeling in your body that is typically associated with love, where you don't want to know the future or change the past and are just content and comfortable where you are and with who you are.

When you reach a level of being able to give unconditional love, you become the channel through which it will flow to everyone. True love is an emotion that can't be experienced; it has to be embodied. Think of a new couple who can't take their eyes off each other; in that moment, they aren't thinking about who they hate or wishing anyone negativity. They are too lost in each other to care. In that moment, they not only love each other, but they also love the whole world; everything is rosy, bright, and positive. This is the state of love that spiritual masters embody and that we must eventually return to, where love for one becomes oneness with all.

Be receptive to the Universe; ask it to transmit the feeling of love to you. Soon, your whole being will be filled with love. Affirm "I am loving" and ask the Universe to let you become aware of and feel the unconditional love flowing through you.

Once you start loving yourself, you accept yourself completely — in whichever situation or state you are in. You realize that you are whole, perfect, strong, powerful, and loving. First, repeat all the affirmations and visualizations in their given order, and then include 'I am loving.'

The Sixth Positive

6

I AM HARMONIOUS

What Does 'Harmony' Mean?

There is a deep, subtle rhythm, equilibrium, and poise in the universe. Everything in nature moves in perfect harmony with each other. The seasons follow each other in a set order, and the full moon follows its cycle of waxing and waning. The sun rises and sets, day moves into night, and night moves into day.

Similarly, humanity too is designed to constantly be in harmony with itself and the rest of Creation. Human life has a certain rhythm of highs and lows in all its spheres. Left alone, it will follow its natural, harmonious cycle of transitioning between the ups and downs of life.

However, as humans, it is our conditioned nature

to keep interfering with the natural order of things and imposing our will on every situation. Due to this, we resist the lows and struggle to hold on to the highs. This constant fight against the design of life is what makes us lose our harmony, not only with each other but also with ourselves.

When animals roam the great plains of Africa, they know that predators are lurking around and that there is a possibility that their young ones will be killed. They are aware of the danger, but they don't live their life in constant fear. You will see them eating, playing, and carrying on with the circle of life. Even with a constant, imminent threat of death, they retain their ability to be joyful. This is possible only because they are in harmony with life and all the events it may bring their way.

On the other side, you see lions hunting down their prey. They will only kill when they are hungry and, even then, only as much as is required. They do not massacre entire species of animals to stock up on food for the future, even though they know they may have to go without food for days in the winter months. This is because they too are in harmony with nature and its changing seasons.

Compare this with our behavior as humans: Our survival (in most cases) is already taken care of, yet we are constantly anxious about the future, worrying about the present, and obsessing over the past. We have restless nights and troubled days, all because we are in disharmony with life and constantly rallying against it.

We may think that it is the events in our life that break our harmony, but actually, it is our response to them that determines our inner state. You may have seen someone go through a terrible illness or tragedy and come out stronger. On the other hand, you may have also known a student who couldn't take the routine pressure of exams and succumbed to it. The situations most of us face are similar in one way or another, but it is the way we deal with them that decides the outcome of the situation and sets the course for our future.

One of the most common ways to get back in touch with nature and in harmony with the world is through the universal life force — the breath. A simple breathing exercise is given in the visualization section below and can help you pause and take a moment to re-center and re-harmonize yourself before you take any action.

Are We Really Harmonious?

To invite harmonious conditions in our life, we must go back to having a harmonious mental attitude. Harmony arises when there is an integration of the different facets of our being. It is that state where our mind, thoughts, emotions, reason, and feelings are all in alignment.

All children (including ourselves when we were younger) are harmonious. They say what they think and do what they wish. There is no pretense, expectation, or judgment. They always live in the present moment and, therefore, find it very easy to switch from sadness to happiness or from doubt to excitement. They flow in harmony with their inner self as well as the outer universe. Thus, they are always happy, loved, and at ease.

It is only as we grow up that we lose this harmonious nature and try to align ourselves to superficial ideologies of what we *should* do, think or be, instead of following our inner compass and simply doing, thinking, and being.

Children go through more difficulties than adults do; they don't know how to eat, walk, or even talk. As some people become old, they once again forget how to do these things. Yet, a baby is seen as adorable and an old person is seen as incapable. Why?

One of the reasons is that children don't view themselves as incapable. They are so in harmony with life that they trust they will always be taken care of. They are confident that they can achieve anything, and they are joyful in the face of adversity. Whereas old people have had a lifetime of conditioning and are scared of being a burden. They are regretful of events that happened in their past and feel hopeless in the face of their future. Their emotions create disharmony between their mind and their body, and put them out of sync with life. You must have known people who, even in their old age, despite their illness, have remained active, joyful, and excited about the future. Which type of old person is better off in life? The one who is in disharmony with their situation or the one who is in harmony with it?

By reciting the affirmation 'I am harmonious,' we invite the child within us to emerge once again. We will stop taking life seriously and recognize that the highs and lows are merely alternating cycles of life. This knowledge will help us stay calm during the lows and centered during the highs.

Method of Visualization

When right thought accompanied by right reasoning is followed by right words to produce right action, then they all move in tandem to produce the desired outcome. An even and balanced flow of thoughts and emotions signify equilibrium in our personality and put us in harmony with the rest of Creation. Think of the harmony, rhythm, order, and equilibrium of the universe. These right thoughts should develop into a feeling, and that feeling should be deeply ingrained in our heart and mind so that we can access it anytime.

You may have heard the advice to take a deep breath when you were scared or nervous. This is because breath is a powerful tool to put you back in synchronicity with nature and the universe.

Close your eyes and take twelve deep breaths. After you inhale, pause, hold for a moment, and then slowly exhale. Pause again; don't rush to take in another breath. Once you are ready, inhale and repeat.

If you do this exercise thrice a day, in a few days, you will start to notice the difference in your mind and life. Suddenly, you may feel connected to the world and realize that the universe will take care of you. You will see that if you are moving in this orderly manner, you are in harmony with the external, internal, eternal, and unchangeable laws of nature. You are in a state of *ananda* (bliss) and, therefore, creating an energy field around you that uplifts everyone and everything. You will be creating harmony wherever you go. You will develop a nonjudgmental and non-reactive attitude toward every situation and a gracious acceptance of what *is*.

If you are whole, perfect, strong, powerful, and loving, you will naturally also be harmonious. Practice the affirmations and visualizations in the same order, and you will manifest their truth in your life.

The Seventh Positive

7

I AM RICH

What Does 'Richness' Mean?

When we hear the word 'rich,' we probably think of big mansions, fancy cars, and a lavish lifestyle. While these images are not incorrect, they represent only material richness. However, there is another type of richness that is not often spoken about but is highly valued just the same — the richness of spirit.

To be rich in spirit means that we are generous with our time, energy, goodwill, or whatever else may be asked of us. We are unafraid to let life flow freely from us. This means that when someone asks us for our time so that we may listen to them and provide guidance, requests us to devote our efforts and energies toward a noble cause, or even simply tells us to send goodwill and good wishes toward the fulfillment of their dreams, we don't hold back and, instead, choose to support them in whatever way we can.

We often hear that a certain person has a 'generous heart' or a 'big heart.' This means that the person does not hold back from giving what they have and what is required in any particular situation. They are rich not only in giving but also in humbly receiving whatever the moment offers them and spontaneously expressing their gratitude. This is very important as we often see people shy away from receiving praise, recognition, or accolades. The reason is that they are living in duality: On one hand, they think of themselves as the doer of their actions; that is, they credit their actions to their ego. On the other hand, they refuse to accept praise because they think that it will fuel their ego, having heard that praising the ego is wrong.

However, someone who is rich in spirit also understands that there is a difference between their ego (that separates them from the world), and their spirit (that unites them with the world). They recognize themselves as being one with the rest of the world and know that by helping others, they are receiving more love, gratitude, and abundance than they ever could have otherwise. Imagine you are stuck on an empty highway at night with a punctured tire. You are scared, hungry, and all alone. The few trucks that pass by are speeding so fast that they do not see you. Sometime later, a truck finally stops, and the driver gets out. He is a kind man and offers to help you. He gives you a sealed bottle of water along with a fresh packet of biscuits. After you eat, he helps you replace your tire. Think of how grateful you will feel toward this man — not just at that moment or for that trip but for years to come as you replay this story to your family and friends. Think of how it will make you view the world differently as a kinder, safer place, and how, perhaps, next time when you're driving on a highway, you will be more aware so that you don't miss someone else who may be in need like you were. The truck driver will receive your blessings for the rest of his life as well as the blessings of all those who hear the story or are helped someday because of it. In giving, he has, in fact, received.

A person who is rich in spirit knows that they have not acted from the ego but, rather, from the spirit. So when they are praised for their actions, they offer that praise to their spirit and humbly bow down before it. They are grateful that they had a chance to serve and look forward to serving again.

If we give freely, we are creating an abundance of richness for ourselves.

Are We Really Rich?

Humans are a part of nature, and nature is the very embodiment of richness. Its natural law is change and abundance. It keeps re-creating and re-birthing itself. Think of a mango tree that produces lots of mangoes when its season comes. And every mango comes with a seed so that it can birth an entire mango tree by itself if the conditions are right. Similarly, a female dog may give birth to up to twelve puppies, each of whom will be able to give birth to twelve more puppies when their time comes. All of nature reflects an image of abundance and not scarcity.

However, in the human kingdom, because we not only view ourselves as separate from the rest of the world but also as separate from each other, we become focused on individual accumulation and display. We want to hoard everything — money, resources, and even the time and energy of our loved ones. We are so focused on 'getting' that we forget what we already have.

Our definition of wealth is relative to our surroundings and keeps shifting to ensure that we are never fully satisfied. For example, Rahul is eager to buy a house in a fancy new building and show off his wealth to the people in his old neighborhood. But once he starts living in the new building, he finds that the children there go to international schools and look down upon his children who go to state-run schools. Somehow, he manages to afford the fees to send his children to the best international school in the city. Then he realizes that everyone else's children are being dropped off in fancy cars, and they make fun of his small car. By the time he can buy a better car, the conversation has shifted to yet another topic or brand. He is exhausted, demotivated, and starts to think of himself as worthless or 'less than.' You can see how, despite earning and achieving so much, he never considers himself 'rich.'

The word 'richness,' as we typically define it, is an illusion, but it doesn't have to be so. Compare Rahul with a simple man in the village who knows his crops are growing well and the yield this year will be good. He wants to go home on time and eat the meal his wife has lovingly cooked for him, and he is eager to show his children the kite he found by the roadside. He is happy and content. He considers himself rich because he has a family, friends, and food on the table.

If we were to define 'being rich,' we would probably say it is a state where all our wants can be fulfilled. But since our wants are never-ending and always changing, the concept of 'richness' always remains an illusion for us. If we could modify or reign in our wants, simply by not comparing ourselves to others, then we would realize that, perhaps, we are already rich.

Method of Visualization

Visualize the life and world you want for yourself. Fill it with abundance, and then recognize it as yours. For instance, picture yourself living in your dream house with the people you love. Your favorite food is laid out on the table, and the room is rich with the sound of laughter and the feeling of togetherness. You are rich in spirit, knowing that everything you say or want will be taken care of for you by the Universe. There is a feeling of surety and permanence to this richness; it will never be taken away from you. Let this visualization sink in, and believe that you can manifest it for yourself.

Using the visualization mentioned above as an aid, think of what being rich would feel like for you, and then try to bring that feeling into your current day-to-day life.

Understand that every thought has the potential to actualize itself. The law of nature is to reflect our thoughts and beliefs to us. This has been explained in the previous chapters when we spoke about one thought attracting multiple other similar thoughts and then affecting outcomes or situations in the external world. Thus, we can partake in the creation of our own future, which has the full potential to reflect the abundance and richness that we desire.

Nature gives us in abundance without any questions asked and without discrimination or expectation. Yet in no way does it get depleted. In the same way, with all the resources available to you, keep affirming "I am rich," and you *will* be rich. By 'rich' it is meant that whenever any needy person comes to you and you are in a position to meet his need by way of offering money, compassion, or your time, you give it. You realize that you have nothing to lose; on the contrary, you only stand to gain. If you don't hold back and give of yourself generously, a constant inflow and outflow will be maintained (as explained above with the example of the truck driver), and you will become a channel through which positive energy keeps flowing.

Practice the visualizations and the affirmations for being whole, perfect, strong, powerful, loving, harmonious, and then for being rich.

The Eighth Positive

8

I AM YOUNG

What Does 'Youthfulness' Mean?

A young-at-heart outlook springs from our attitude toward life and has nothing to do with our chronological age. If our attitude is one of cheerfulness and adopting a creative interest in life, we will feel young even at the age of eighty. A childlike enthusiasm and interest in everything we do can help us not only stay young in spirit but also make us appear youthful physically. We may have come across people who look far younger than their age (without cosmetic modifications). On the other hand, we may also know children who, perhaps, have seen far too much negativity for their young age and already look old or worn out.

However, despite seeing these examples around

us, we view old age as inevitable and not as a point of view. This is because as a result of the interactions with people and the environment around us, our mind passes on information about age-related changes to our subconscious mind, which, in turn, manifests them for us in our external life. (We have discussed in previous chapters how the subconscious mind stores information and decides our life since it is the bulk of the metaphorical iceberg hidden beneath our conscious mind.) For example, we may believe that we will have to wear spectacles by the time we are forty years old or that our knees will give way by the time we reach sixty. It is this belief that makes these eventualities come true for us even if they were avoidable to begin with.

Does this mean that all problems and effects of old age are concocted by the subconscious mind? Of course not. It simply means that, very often, the extent and severity of these effects are in our hands, and we can choose how much we would like to let them affect us. Think of it this way: Two old women go through knee replacement surgeries. The process of recovery (of walking again) is extremely painful. One woman thinks that there is no point in going through so much additional pain; she thinks she is too weak and will die soon anyway. The other woman keeps up with the process of recovery though she cries each time she tries to take a step; she wants to walk normally again so that she can keep visiting her children who are settled abroad. Eventually, her knees heal, and she can walk properly again. Imagine that these women go on to live for another fifteen years. One is bedridden, and the other is traveling the world. Which one will appear more youthful? The situation they were placed in was the same; it was their mind that decided whether it would cause them to age faster or slower.

The subconscious mind, which acts without reasoning, is the architect as well as the maintenance engineer of the body. This means that it can't differentiate between the good information and the bad information that is passed on to it. It blindly acts on our beliefs, whether we realize it or not. The net result is that it maintains the body according to the information absorbed by it, and so we end up creating 'old age' for ourselves.

Are We Really Young?

Science has proved that the cells in our body are constantly regenerating themselves. Thus, at regular intervals, we have a 'new' body with young cells. The only barrier is our mind, which accepts 'aging' and its related complications, thereby manifesting them for us. Hence, if we can change our attitude toward life, we can stay youthful. For instance, you will see *yogis* who look far younger than their chronological age. This is not only because they adopt certain practices to remain youthful; it is because they let life flow.

We are the trustees of our body, so we have to see, speak, hear, and eat in such a way that our body remains beautiful and youthful. Our thoughts have the power to direct our subconscious mind. We can use them to ionize every particle of our being and rejuvenate the cells of our body to acquire the qualities of youth, health, and happiness.

Our subconscious mind will believe all that you tell it and function accordingly. We simply have to do away with negativity and establish positivity within us.

The Indian Advaita sage Nisargadatta Maharaj has said, "Sitting in meditation helps the consciousness to blossom. It causes deeper understanding and spontaneous change in behavior. These changes are brought about in the consciousness itself, not in the pseudo personality. Forced changes are at the level of the mind. Mental and intellectual changes are totally unnatural and different from the ones that take place in the birth principle. These take place naturally, automatically, by themselves due to meditation." A simple meditation exercise to help us remain youthful is given in the visualization section below.

Method of Visualization

To get out of the cycle of repeating the same blueprint of aging and decay, we have to change it. The belief that we create for ourselves delivers the new blueprint that will influence our life. One way to recreate the blueprint is to go to sleep feeling youthful, and we will eventually succeed in implanting the idea of youthfulness in our subconscious mind.

If our mind is clear about aging, then we will not age before our time. Instead of looking ten years older than our chronological age, we will look ten years younger. With this understanding and with the practice of affirming and meditating upon the words 'I am young,' we will generate the power of that thought. The rest will then be taken care of by our Highest Self.

When we dwell on the word 'young,' we have to concentrate on various aspects of youthfulness, such as always being ready for adventure, being excited to try out new things and meet new people, being joyful and ambitious about the future, as well as being willing to change and let go. We should use our creative imagination to visualize that our face, in fact, our whole being, is glowing and radiant.

Try this meditation exercise: Close your eyes and sit in a relaxed position. Bring an image of yourself as youthful, the way you would like to look, at the center of your mind. Hold this image as long as you can, and then let it gently fade (it will sink into the subconscious mind). From there, it will work at slowly rewiring your body to reflect youth instead of old age.

There is also another way to do the same exercise: Stand in front of a mirror and look at yourself. See yourself as you currently are — without judgment and without creating a story in your mind. (*Oh! When I was younger, I used to be so fit. Now I hardly get any time to exercise.* Or *These dark circles look horrible. I should apply something to them.*) Look yourself squarely into your eyes with a quiet mind.

Slowly, start to alter your reflection in your mind, based on your interpretation of the word 'young.' You may remember yourself twenty years earlier, when your eyes were brighter or you stood a little taller. See that image reflected in the mirror in front of you.

Close your eyes and imagine yourself walking into the mirror and merging with the image you see; the person you currently are is merging with the person you would like to be. For example, the Rita of today, with her gray hair, baggy clothes, or tired eyes is merging with her ideal image of youth from twenty years ago, when she had lustrous hair and joyful eyes, and wore stylish clothes. Or the Chris of today, with his stress lines visible on his forehead, stiff posture, and boring clothes is merging with the carefree version of Chris who was relaxed, happy, and youthful in his outlook on life.

Leave the old version of yourself behind; say goodbye to it. When you open your eyes, feel as if you are stepping back from the mirror as the young, hopeful, happy, and carefree person you once were. You are leaving behind all signs of aging. You no longer want to be that old person who replaced your younger self. You are young again.

Keep repeating the affirmation 'I am young,' till it sinks into the depths of your body and starts to physically remodel it to reflect perpetual youth. With this meditation, you will break through all negative conditioning (regarding aging) forced into your mind by the traditional thought patterns of your cultural background.

When you practice all affirmations and their corresponding visualizations in order, then you will start to embody a being who is whole, perfect, strong, powerful, loving, harmonious, rich, and young.

The Ninth Positive

9

I AM HAPPY

What Does 'Happiness' Mean?

We all have our personal definition of happiness. Usually, we associate happiness with the fulfillment of our desires. We feel that if we had more than enough in each area of our life (e.g., more money, a bigger house, and robust good health), we would be happy.

Yet, true happiness is in being at peace with ourselves and with the world. If we base our happiness on the fulfillment of our desires, it would be very fleeting and fragile because our desires never end. True happiness is a more permanent state of being, and its permanence depends on the fact that it stems from within us and not outside us.

It is important to understand that, ultimately,

the events outside us are not in our control: we can't singlehandedly eradicate the coronavirus pandemic, ask our loved ones who have passed away to come back to life, or change an answer on a test after we have submitted it. But our attitude toward these events is in our hands. Since happiness is so important to us, it makes sense to define it based on the quality of our inner life more than our outer one.

However, this is possible only when our body, mind, and spirit vibrate in unison, which is not something that will happen of its own accord. We will have to work at it consciously by integrating the five senses and taking charge of our inner life. In other words, when we are able to respond to a situation with awareness and not as a knee-jerk reaction, only then will we be able to maintain our state of happiness. There is a story that perfectly illustrates this:

Two boys, Raj and Sumit, grow up in an abusive home with an alcoholic father. They run away when they are teenagers and get separated along the way.

Many years later, a common childhood friend, Prem, happens to meet Raj on the road. He sees that Raj has also become an alcoholic just like his father. He spends his day begging for money and his nights passed out on footpaths outside shady bars. He can't talk without slurring and constantly abuses the world. Raj explains, "My father was an abusive alcoholic. I had to turn out like him."

Some months later, the same friend bumps into Sumit who is living in another city. He has a beautiful wife, three teenage children, a lovely mansion, and a well-paying job. He has never had alcohol or uttered a swear word in his life. Sumit explains, "My father was an abusive alcoholic. I could have never turned out like him."

This poignant story illustrates that while the events in our life may not have been in our control, our reaction to them is. And depending on how we respond to the situations and people we encounter, we have a chance to decide if we will invite happiness into our present as well as future or remain stuck in the dead past.

Are We Really Happy?

True happiness lies within us. This state can be achieved when our emotional, mental, and physical bodies are in balance: when what we think, what we say, and what we do are in harmony with each other. This feeling of happiness is more than just an experience of momentary joy and pleasure; it is a state of mind in which a person is always happy.

We arrive at this state when we have moved beyond the mind and become an observer or a witness of the transitory phases of life. In other words, we cease to identify with the mind and live more consciously. For example, in the above story, both boys grew up with a difficult father. Raj identified with the father and thought that if his father was an alcoholic, it meant that alcoholism was in his genes and that he had no choice but to be like him. Perhaps he also thought that he was a bad person and so deserved the hardships in his childhood. This made him feel as if the rest of his life would also be similarly and deservedly bad. On the other hand, Sumit looked at the situation as a witness. He observed that while it was a difficult situation, it did not reflect on him or define his future. He chose to live his life consciously so as not to make the same mistakes his father did, especially since he had seen the pain and suffering his father's alcoholism had caused those around him.

Similarly, we too can choose to leave behind the negative situations of our past, view them as stepping stones toward our growth, and be happy with everything life has given us. To acquire this mindset, we need to be determined, practice meditation, and lead a holistic lifestyle. This will ensure that our mind, energy, and effort are all going in the same direction — toward permanent happiness.

The revered Indian sage Sri Ramana Maharshi has said, "You can have, or rather, you will yourself be, the highest imaginable kind of happiness. All other kinds of happiness which you have spoken of as 'pleasure,' 'joy,' 'happiness,' 'bliss' are only reflections of the ananda, which, in your true nature, you are."

Method of Visualization

In meditation, when no thoughts are occurring, then the mind is clear and tranquil; it becomes a gateway to living consciously and ultimate transformation.

In the early hours of the morning, when no thoughts are cluttering the mind and before the day's activities have begun, it is the best time to practice meditation. It is for these early hours of the morning that the Indian sage Swami Ramanathan has given a very powerful exercise.

He advises you to dress with particular care, as if you were going to meet someone whose opinion matters very much to you. Then follow the next steps:

1. Stand before a mirror.
2. Smile at yourself, feel happy inside, and look squarely into your eyes.
3. Start a conversation with yourself. Call yourself by your name and say these statements:
   - (Name), I am deeply grateful to you, for I have learned that you are able to do whatever I wish to do. I have learned to

place absolute trust in you. (Be dramatic. Arouse your emotions. Smile happily at yourself, and feel very happy.)

- My faith in you is unbounded, for all things are possible to you. I have learned that you are what the Creator is. I have discovered what the creative energy in you can do, and it wants to do whatever I direct it to do. (Look deep into your eyes and believe that what you are saying is true. Act as if you are on the verge of some great realization of joy or success, or whatever you have in mind for yourself.)
- You are successful. You will achieve today whatever you set out to achieve, for you have discovered the new power for which there is nothing impossible. (Rouse yourself to a state of joyous emotion. See your eyes shine and look with earnest concentration into their reflection in the mirror. Feel the warmth of love toward yourself and everybody else, declaring that as you will

expect, demand, and receive help from others, you too are prepared to help and serve all of them.)

Start out with this intention. Be kind. Smile at people and then watch. You will be surprised how their response will correspond precisely with your own attitude.

If you so wish, you may change the wording to suit your goals. If you feel like it, you can write down what you will say before actually going through the above exercise. Use the finest, most attractive, and most effective words. Be decisive and make the conversation very positive so that, afterward, you will feel that you have had a very pleasant visit from someone intimately known to you and that you are really happy as a result of it.

The word for the state you will reach is ananda — the blissful state. It is a permanent state of 'being' and not something that comes and goes. In other words, it is the bliss of being.

When you are whole, perfect, strong, powerful, loving, harmonious, rich, and young, then as a direct result, you will be happy.

1

"I Am Whole"

2

"I Am Perfect"

3

"I Am Strong"

4

"I Am Powerful"

5

"I Am Loving"

6

"I Am Harmonious"

7

"I Am Rich"

8

"I Am Young"

9

"I Am Happy"

CONCLUSION

People have a lot of questions about positive as well as negative thoughts and how they should handle them. A simple explanation is given below.

There are two actively operating forces in our life — the positive and the negative. These form our creative currents of love and hate or construction and destruction. The main switch to regulate these forces is thought. Our thoughts are not limited to our mind; thoughts create emotions, which, in turn, give rise to different sensations in our body. For example, we all may experience 'butterflies in the stomach' when we are feeling nervous or a headache when we are feeling stressed. Over time, these sensations can solidify into ill health: headaches can worsen into migraines, suppressed emotions can cause blocks in our arteries, or increased fear can cause a weak digestive system. When we constantly have happy thoughts, we will see the results in the brightness of our eyes, the sharpness of our intellect, and the robust health of our body and mind.

Our entire life is a reflection of our thoughts. The concern, however, is how to retain positive thoughts and reject negative thoughts. We cannot stop negative thoughts from arising, but we can choose to replace them by focusing more on positive and harmonious thoughts. The affirmations play an important role in this. They require constant practice, discipline, and focus. Once we reach a certain level of proficiency in being able to watch our thoughts and in holding on more to positive thoughts, we slowly start moving away from our negative conditioning. We then realize that there is a law of nature that reflects our thoughts and, by holding good thoughts, it is possible to manifest positive situations in our life.

The Word Is God

Just having good thoughts is not enough unless they are verbalized. Words are the conveyors of thoughts. When we utter a word, we become aware of the process that goes on in the mind behind what we are saying. For example, in our mind, we often say the worst things to people we are angry with. However, if we were to say them out loud, we will probably realize how vicious we sound and immediately wish to take them back. This is because when we vocalize our thoughts, we are able to hear them as a third party would. The vocalized words produce feelings in us that enable us to realize the effect of those words on our body, mind, and intellect: Did we feel good after uttering those words, or did we feel ashamed?

We then realize that when we speak the words aloud, we are the creators of what we are declaring. Having created it, we cannot, then, hold back the force that brings what we have created into manifesting itself.

Genesis, the first book of the Bible, begins with

the sentence: "In the beginning was the Word, and the Word was with God, and the Word was God." Keeping this in mind, while articulating a thought, we need to consciously choose the word and the tone in which it is sent forth in order to give it the power and effectiveness to manifest as desired. If we can bring harmony between our thoughts, feelings, words, and actions, then we will be able to materialize our core desires.

Most of our life revolves around the words 'I wish' or 'if only,' as in "I wish my spouse was more like person X" or "If only I was prettier; then everyone would appreciate me more." Both these terms imply that there is a lack within us and in our experience of life. We spend so much of our time focusing on the lack — whether it is lack of beauty, love, success, money, or respect — that we unintentionally manifest more of it.

We Are Bigger than Our Problems

We have discussed before that our subconscious mind doesn't know how to differentiate between good and bad. It simply takes in what our conscious mind is repeating to it and creates our life accordingly. If we keep repeating phrases such as 'I am not good enough' or 'I never get what I want,' we ensure that those statements keep coming true for us. The law of life is simple: it enhances that which you give your attention to.

So what should we do in the moments when we genuinely don't feel good enough or feel terrified that our life won't work out or that everything is falling apart? Should we suppress these feelings and pretend they don't exist? Of course not. Problems are a part of life, and the key words are in that sentence itself: 'a part of.' We must recognize that while problems are a part of life, they are not all of it. Our life is bigger than the difficulties of the present moment, and so are we.

One way for us to step back from the commotion of everyday life and reconnect with our Highest Self is through the daily practice of The Nine Positives.

When we recite the words 'I am,' as in 'I am whole' or 'I am perfect,' we are reminding ourselves that in the present moment, despite the events in our external life, we remain whole, perfect, strong, powerful, loving, harmonious, rich, young, and happy in our inner being. By doing so, we focus on the tangible, beautiful reality of who we are as our Highest Self and the universal qualities that we embody. And naturally, the more we focus on our happiness, love, strength, power, and perfection, the more of these aspects will we be able to manifest and enhance in ourselves and our life.

In the ancient Hindu scripture, the Katha Upanishad, human life has been depicted as an upside-down tree, known as the *Ashvattha* tree, which is said to be perennially evergreen or, in other words, immortal. Just as the roots of a tree go deep down into the earth and spread out to gather nourishment from the soil, similarly the human mind has its roots upwards in the Universal Mind, the source of all possibilities. The connection to the Universal Mind is always open. Once we connect to It, we will be provided with all that we need by transcending the limitations of space and time.

We have discussed before that our subconscious mind is most receptive in the period just before we sleep or during deep meditation. During this time, we may repeat any idea, dream, or thought to it, and it will work toward manifesting that for us. However, there is a word of caution that goes along with this: as mentioned above, most of our thoughts center around lack, and our wishes are constantly changing or modifying themselves.

To prevent us from the futility of chasing empty dreams, wise Tibetan monks gave us The Nine Positives as a guide. The monks recognized that all our desires were ultimately centered on making ourselves feel happy. So instead of taking the long route to illusory happiness (through the fulfillment of our never-ending materialistic desires), they showed us how to manifest happiness directly from within our innermost self.

There is a Chinese curse that says "May all your wishes come true." It is considered a curse because if every wish of yours had come true, your life would have been miserable. Your sibling may have died if you wished death upon them during a childhood fight, you may have divorced your spouse, flung your co-worker from the roof, or swapped your children with your neighbor's. So many times, even with positive wishes, we look back in gratitude that they weren't fulfilled, because something much greater happened for us instead.

Thus, the sensible thing to do is to not make specific demands from life, but instead, ask for the universal qualities of truth, joy, and peace to manifest from within you and spread into each aspect of your life, with the help of The Nine Positives.

Planting the Positives

The Nine Positives are not merely words strung together. They are seeds that will sprout and create within you the values contemplated and expressed in exact proportion to the feelings with which you say the affirmations. They should be affirmed every day, in the order that they are given, with belief, sincerity, and dedication, so that they work in your best interests. Let these affirmations guide your life, and you will never lack again.

If you are still wondering whether The Nine Positives will be able to elicit true transformation from within you, the only way to truly know is to practice them daily and see for yourself. Sit quietly, and try to listen to the answers that emerge from within you. Contemplate the inner meaning of The Nine Positives, and you will gather strength from the simple yet powerfully vibrating affirmations, which cover every aspect of your life.

TESTIMONIALS

In so many of Santosh Ma's teachings, I have found a deep wisdom that underlies the simplicity of her messages, which sometimes seem almost too good to be true. The Nine Positives are no exception to this, and after regularly reciting them for nearly a year now, I can, without doubt, say that they are life-changing and that they really do work.

When I recite them first thing upon waking, they set my day off on the right foot. When I recite them at the end of the day, they help me reframe and integrate whatever events might have transpired during the day.

The trick (I have found) is that they need to be done with regularity so that the seeds that we are planting in our mind have a chance to grow. The result will be an increasingly enjoyable experience of reality, a greater sense of acceptance, and improved harmony in all aspects of one's life.

Mike Medof, USA
Property Manager

I think The Nine Positives should be one of the first things a child should be taught. Their practice is a very powerful tool to help you get in touch with your positive essence.

Since I got introduced to The Nine Positives, they have rescued me from falling into a negative mind frame on several occasions. They made me aware that I was slipping into a detrimental mind frame and became the pivot in helping to change my thought process.

It is not just a blind repetition of statements; rather, it is a realization that each of The Nine Positives is my true nature, waiting to shine forth.

Rashmi Jokhakar, India
Business Consultant

Of all the affirmations in the Brahma Vidya Course [explained in the next chapter, 'The Eight Spiritual Breaths Course'], The Nine Positives are the ones I initially found very difficult to relate to. This was because years of conditioning had led me to think and believe that I was a poor, limited, imperfect self, which always put me in a state of lack.

After almost two years of practicing The Nine Positives, the meaning of 'wholeness' (and the subsequent positives that follow) suddenly dawned on me. I realized that wholeness is something to which nothing can (or needs to) be added or subtracted. The sense of lack disappears, and we realize that we are (and always have been) complete and perfect the way we are. This diminishes the mental drive to become something other than the wholesome self we are. The feeling that follows this realization is one of utter elation.

Ramesh Venugopal, USA
Physicist

The Nine Positives gave me an important understanding of the attributes and facets of a wholesome life.

I realized that spiritual growth or life evolution for any aspirant involves deconditioning and reprogramming their consciousness. The affirmations in The Nine Positives are empowered like mantras and they work to reprogram our consciousness on a core level.

The Nine Positives also gave me a sense that, eventually, the spiritual path leads to us becoming whole, powerful, loving, strong, and happy. These are the outcomes of balanced living and spiritual evolution.

Konark Bhandari, India
Business Development Executive

It has been my privilege to study The Nine Positives under Santosh Ma. The practice is extremely powerful.

By practicing The Nine Positives for some time, I have felt a lot of difference within myself. I have realized that they work at the deepest levels of our body, and the changes they bring are positive as well as permanent. The whole personality changes: the outlook becomes positive, and one feels a lot of energy within — both mental as well as physical. To start with, one is able to overcome any negative attitude that one has.

The Nine Positives have made me more open and articulate. When, for example, I say "I am powerful — all-powerful," I am able to feel that power within me, and that gives me a lot of confidence.

I am ever grateful to Santosh Ma for this great gift that she has showered on all her students, including me. She is very loving and wonderful. I am blessed to have her in my life.

Sunita Tiwari, India
Astrologer

With consistent practice, The Nine Positives have started to make much more sense to me. Previously, the terms 'whole,' 'perfect,' 'strong,' 'powerful,' 'loving,' 'harmonious,' 'rich,' 'young,' and 'happy' used to have textbook meanings for me; that is, I used to mechanically read what was written without understanding it, like a child memorizing the words in a textbook for an exam, without understanding them. However, these words resonate with me now, and I know them to be my deepest truth.

The practice of these affirmations is perfection too as the removal of layers from our past conditioning helps. The awareness of 'what is' becomes more important than what can or should be.

When I read about the positives, the feeling was more on the ego, the 'I,' as all the positives have an 'I' to begin with. Yet as one becomes more aware of the wholeness within, the way you even use and speak 'I' changes. The world outside seems whole and perfect the way it is; in fact, the idea of 'being perfect' changes.

As you start observing, more and more, the intuitive power to see the play of emotions coming up naturally flows. Hence, the urge to react to a feeling of being angry, upset, or fearful, or to any known or unknown situation or person is not judged by you as right or wrong. I also see that connection when I read of *gunas*, as defined in the Bhagavad Gita.

In any given situation, I choose to be honest with myself, take my time, and speak my truth. It's not about being right or wrong; it's about being truthful and harmonious within. The rest, somehow, falls into place as you feel rich with the bounty of resources within you.

True to every word, the affirmations work within as you consciously start being more aware of yourself. Once that space is understood, you listen to your body, mind, and intellect as they start to function in harmony.

As you feel wholeness within, you see the same outside too. That is how The Nine Positives have worked for me.

Vandna Soni, India
Homemaker

The Nine Positives are a complete set of very powerful affirmations. They encompass every aspect of our life. The affirmations, with their visualizations, can help manifest everything that one desires. They are a beautiful and positive way to align one's life.

Emotively reciting The Nine Positives as often as you can, sends a strong message to you of well-being. They have helped dispel my doubts and fears, and I am more balanced and confident in every aspect of my life.

Sanjay Vaid, India
Businessman

THE EIGHT SPIRITUAL BREATHS COURSE

The Nine Positives are derived from an ancient Tibetan practice of breathing exercises and affirmations, which is known in India as the Brahma Vidya Course. The story behind the origins of this course, along with the author Santosh Sachdeva's journey in studying and, subsequently, expanding this course, is given below.

Origins of the Brahma Vidya Course

According to legend, Padmasambhava, a renowned yogi and teacher at the ancient Nalanda University, foresaw the destruction of the university by foreign invaders and, hence, migrated to Tibet with a select group of disciples. From there, he continued to share his knowledge and guide deserving students on the path of self-discovery. Among his teachings were a set of powerful breathing exercises and affirmations that were designed to help individuals realize their highest potential.

Many decades later, in the early 1900s, Edwin John Dingle, a young English journalist, traveled to Tibet and studied the same exercises under a Tibetan master (possibly one of the disciples in Padmasambhava's lineage). Later known as Ding Le Mei to over 220,000 students, he then spread this teaching (he called it Mental Physics) throughout the USA and the world through the institute he established in California, USA.

The practice of these breathing exercises was revived and conducted in India under the aegis of The Brahma Vidya Mission founded by Swami K. S. Ramanathan, who had studied the course under Ding Le Mei. Swami Ramanathan visited the Mental Physics headquarters at Yucca Valley, USA, where Ding Le Mei's wife gave him the title 'Jyotirmayananda (Being of Light).'

I joined the course in 1995 under the guidance

of my *guru*, Justice M. L. Dudhat, who had studied the course under Swami Ramanathan.

Until recently, Brahma Vidya was taught as a course in self-development. It was designed to help aspirants access their unlimited inner potential. The goal of the course was to work toward positive and desirable changes within ourselves, which would provide access to higher knowledge and also fill us with peace, wisdom, and compassion.

My Experience of Practicing the Brahma Vidya Course

Practicing these powerful breathing exercises (there are eight of them) along with their empowered affirmations revealed to me that there is a lot more to human beings than what the external senses can feel or perceive.

I understood that our ego is not our true being. Rather, our true being is the reality that never changes and is not bound by time or space. Thus, it cannot be grasped through the senses or the mind; it can only be experienced. It is self-existent and, therefore, immortal.

My practice of the Brahma Vidya Course took me in a direction that had not been previously experienced or documented by any aspirant. After some prolonged and serious contemplation, it dawned on me that these breathing exercises were designed to activate the *chakras* (the subtle body meridians) which would help an aspirant systematically access the descending and ascending energies of the *Kundalini* (a sleeping, dormant, potent force which lies coiled at the base of the spine). This, in turn, would enable the practitioner to enter the experiential stage where knowledge is gained at the subtle level from subtle dimensions.

This realization led me to bring out a book called *The Eight Spiritual Breaths*, which has detailed descriptions of each 'breath' and the related chakras that they energize. All the insights gained through my experience with the breaths serve as an invaluable guide for the aspirant. This book eventually led to the creation and development of The Eight Spiritual Breaths Course.

Purpose of The Eight Spiritual Breaths Course

The Eight Spiritual Breaths Course is a scientific yogic system of right thinking, breathing, and meditation that can renew our life. It is a further elaboration and refinement of the principles taught in the Brahma Vidya Course. In this course, we delve deeper into the spiritual and subtle aspects of Brahma Vidya, which results in an enriched understanding of our relationship with God and the Universe. As each practitioner's connection to their Divine Intelligence is strengthened, they are guided firmly yet gently on the path of Self-realization, and the subconscious mind is assigned the central role of bringing about physiological and spiritual transformation through the affirmations.

The Eight Spiritual Breaths Course is designed to help aspirants access the unlimited potential lying dormant within them. The course combines instructions for the eight breathing exercises, along with their respective affirmations and guidance for meditation.

The practice of these breaths results in the

enhancement of our creative potential, increased levels of calmness, attainment of robust health, and higher energy levels. The course is a planned, progressive methodology to provide us with the systematic steps required to achieve mastery in our life across all dimensions: physical, mental, emotional, social, familial, financial, aspirational, and spiritual. These constitute the complete matrix of a well-integrated life. In essence, it is designed to ensure that we beat to the rhythm of the Universe.

The breaths allow us to clear deep-seated memories and blocks from our past lives, and traumas suffered by the cells of the physical body as well as the mental, emotional, and etheric bodies. They help us work through the deepest parts of our subconscious and unconscious blocks, with grace and ease. We can then live the life we are meant to live by achieving our highest potential, thereby fulfilling our purpose in life.

Regular practitioners and adherents of The Eight Spiritual Breaths Course have attested to being infused with more vigor and becoming more focused, compassionate, patient, loving, introspective, and sensitive to the higher energies. This opens the gateway to increased levels of awareness in their daily life. The breaths infuse us with more *prana*, the divine consciousness, which will bring about the transformation we need in our mind, body, and life. Prana is the divine vehicle to attain the highest levels of consciousness in the physical body.

We can readily access and take advantage of this spiritual and scientific practice, which is now made available and easy to follow. To reach seekers far and wide, it is now also available as an online self-study course, with all relevant material made available to support you in your practice.

In Keeping with the Growing Evolution of Human Consciousness

The basic Brahma Vidya Course, under the guidance of the late Justice M. L. Dudhat, has now evolved to a different level of experience. Human awareness is today making rapid breakthroughs in accessing new dimensions of consciousness. As Brahma Vidya is a science of evolution, it has to be kept updated and in harmony with the developing consciousness. This is precisely the role envisaged by The Eight Spiritual Breaths Course.

I am grateful to have received the sanction as well as the blessings of both Swami Ramanathan and my guru, Justice Dudhat, for the publishing of my book *The Eight Spiritual Breaths*, on which the course is based.

Please visit www.eightspiritualbreaths.com to learn more about the course.

Santosh Sachdeva

BIBLIOGRAPHY

The 9 Positives is based on the book *Brahma Vidya — An Ancient System of Yoga and Philosophy* by Swami Ramanathan (Guru Jyotirmayananda) as well as lectures on the Brahma Vidya Course by Justice M. L. Dudhat.

Other References

Dingle, Edwin J. *Breathing Your Way to Youth*. Whitefish: Kessinger Publishing, 1998.

Haanel, Charles F. *The Master Key System*. St. Louis: Psychology Publishing; New York: The Master Key Institute, 1916.

Moritz, Andreas. *Timeless Wisdom*. Ener-Chi.com, 2013.

Mudaliar, A. Devaraja. *Day by Day with Bhagavan*. Tiruvannamalai: Sri Ramanasramam, 2011.

Murphy, Dr. Joseph. *The Power of Your Subconscious Mind*. Mumbai: Embassy Books, 2010.

Wattles, Wallace D. *The Science of Getting Rich*. Mumbai: Yogi Impressions, 2017.

For information on The Eight Spiritual Breaths,
visit: www.eightspiritualbreaths.com

For information on Santosh Sachdeva,
visit: www.santoshsachdeva.com

For further details, contact:
Yogi Impressions LLP
1711, Centre 1, World Trade Centre,
Cuffe Parade, Mumbai 400 005, India.

Fill in the Mailing List form on our website
and receive, via email, information on
books, authors, events and more.
Visit: www.yogiimpressions.com

Telephone: (022) 4011 5981, 2215 5036
E-mail: yogi@yogiimpressions.com

Join us on Facebook:
www.facebook.com/yogiimpressions

Join us on Instagram:
www.instagram.com/yogi_impressions

ALSO PUBLISHED BY YOGI IMPRESSIONS

English

Hindi

Marathi

Gujarati

The Eight Spiritual Breaths

Breathing Exercises and Affirmations that transform your life

by Santosh Sachdeva

After migrating to Tibet, the renowned yogi and teacher, Padmasambhava of Nalanda University, developed a set of Breathing Exercises to help human beings actualize their highest potential. Eventually this course came to India and was taught in Mumbai where the author completed it under the guidance of a spiritual teacher. In *The Eight Spiritual Breaths*, she brings a modern perspective to these Breathing Exercises and shows how they can help spiritual aspirants to gain mastery across all dimensions – in their life.

The Eight Spiritual Breaths can help you to:

- Improve memory retention
- Enhance creative potential
- Increase states of calmness
- Revitalise health and energy levels
- Attain personal goals with ease

ALSO PUBLISHED BY YOGI IMPRESSIONS

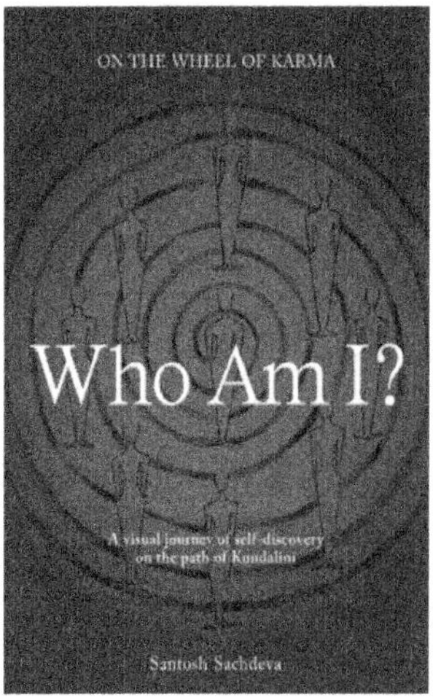

The Sacred India Tarot

Inspired by Indian Mythology and Epics

78 cards + 4 bonus cards + 350 page handbook

The Sacred India Tarot is truly an offering from India to the world. It is the first and only Tarot deck that works solely within the parameters of sacred Indian mythology – almost the world's only living mythology today.

Printed in Great Britain
by Amazon

49497059R00086